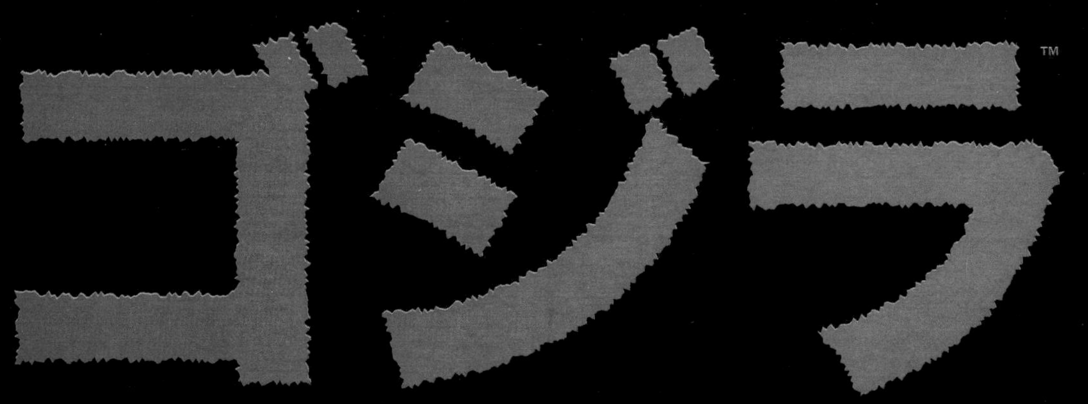

WRITER
DUANE SWIERCZYNSKI

ARTIST
SIMON GANE

COLORIST
RONDA PATTISON

LETTERER / CREATIVE CONSULTANT
CHRIS MOWRY

EDITOR
BOBBY CURNOW

COVER ARTWORK BY ARTHUR ADAMS
COVER COLORS BY PETER DOHERTY
COLLECTION EDITS BY JUSTIN EISINGER AND ALONZO SIMON
COLLECTION DESIGN BY CHRIS MOWRY

MEXICO CITY
TODAY IS SUPPOSED TO BE THE HAPPIEST DAY OF HIS LIFE.

IRVING "URV" JASSIM IS LEAVING BEHIND A LIFE OF VIOLENCE...

...FOR HIS ONE TRUE LOVE.

BUT OF COURSE, VIOLENCE HAS A WAY OF FINDING YOU ANYWAY.

OFTEN IN THE WAY YOU LEAST EXPECT IT.

THOUGH URV IS A MAN OF VIOLENCE, THE FAMILY AND FRIENDS GATHERED HERE TODAY ARE NOT.
THEY ARE ILL-PREPARED AND ESSENTIALLY DEFENSELESS.
JUST LIKE EDUARDO.
URV, HOWEVER, IS A MAN WHO USED TO PRIDE HIMSELF ON BEING PREPARED FOR ANY SITUATION, NO MATTER HOW HOPELESS OR HORRIFIC.
IT IS A SKILL SET HE PROMISED EDUARDO HE WOULD NEVER USE AGAIN.
SOMEWHERE IN HIS FEVERED MIND, URV TELLS HIMSELF THIS ACT IS NOT A BETRAYAL.
FOR HIM, IT IS MERELY ACCOUNTING. THE LOSS OF HIS ONE TRUE LOVE MUST BE REPAID.
FZZZ

THROOOOM

ALAS...

...IT IS AN INEQUITY THAT WILL HAVE TO BE SETTLED ANOTHER DAY.

THE ATTACKS ARE NOT CONFINED TO MEXICO, HOWEVER.
THESE DAYS WERE SUPPOSED TO BE DEDICATED TO GLOBAL RENEWAL AND REBUILDING.
BUT ALL OVER THE WORLD, IN PEACEFUL CITIES...
AUTÓDROMO JOSÉ CARLOS PACE, BRAZIL
...AND MILITARY BASES ALIKE, THE GIANT MONSTERS ARE RISING ONCE AGAIN.
YONGSAN GARRISON, SEOUL, SOUTH KOREA

INCLUDING THE MOST FEARSOME OF THEM ALL...

FIFTY MILES OUTSIDE WASHINGTON, D.C.

FORTY STORIES OF SHEER TERROR
BOXER.
PROFESSIONAL: SOLDIER.
AMATEUR: COOK.
CURRENT STATUS: MAKING POACHED EGGS.
TRYING TO, ANYWAY.
THE HELL?

GAH!

BOXER IS EX-BRITISH SPECIAL FORCES. HARDEST OF THE HARDBOILED.

HE HAS A KNACK FOR SURVIVING THE WORST HELLHOLES ON EARTH AND SCRAMBLING OUT OF IMPOSSIBLE SITUATIONS.

WHICH PROBABLY OVERQUALIFIES HIM AS A BODYGUARD, BUT BOXER LIKES THE PAY AND THE ACCESS TO FANCY KITCHENS.
HE ALSO COULDN'T REFUSE TO PROTECT A TEENAGED GIRL.
MISS MURAKAMI!

OH, NO.
NOT BLOODY YOU.

1 Departure

DUDE... WHY ARE YOU MAKING SO MUCH NOISE?
GRAB YOUR THINGS, MISS MURAKAMI. WE HAVE TO GO RIGHT NOW.
BOXER'S CLIENT IS THE DAUGHTER OF A JAPANESE BILLIONAIRE, IN TOWN FOR TALKS ABOUT BANKROLLING THE RECONSTRUCTION OF WASHINGTON, D.C.
WHAT TIME IS IT ANYWAY? OH, YOU ARE SO GETTING FIRED.
AS A SHOW OF FAITH, THE BILLIONAIRE HERSELF MOVED INTO THE PENTHOUSE FLOOR OF THIS NEW, SUPPOSEDLY GIANT-MONSTER-PROOF TOWER.
ALONG WITH HER 15-YEAR-OLD DAUGHTER, GWEN.

BOXER HAS NEVER FAILED AN ASSIGNMENT.
EVER.
THIS IS WHAT BOXER EXCELS AT...

...THE WORST HELLHOLES ON EARTH...
OH MY GOD OH MY GOD OH MY GOD—
—MY GOD OH MY GOD OH MY GOD OH—

... AND IMPOSSIBLE SITUATIONS.

BOXER, WHAT THE *HELL* ARE YOU DO—
AAAAIIEEEEEEE!
THRO
OOM
BANG
THUD
THUD
THUD
THUD
THUD
THUD

WE'LL BE SAFE IN HERE... RIGHT?
IF A BUILDING'S GOING TO FALL, THE FIRE TOWERS ARE DESIGNED TO BE THE LAST THINGS TO GO.
YOUR MOM SAID THIS IS A NEW BUILDING, LATEST SAFETY FEATURES AND ALL, MEANT TO BE GIANT MONSTER-PR—
BOXER KNEW THE FOUR WALLS AROUND THEM WOULDN'T LAST MUCH LONGER.
FIRE EXIT
BANG
THEY NEEDED A WAY DOWN... AND OUT.
FLOOR 36
THE POWER'S OUT! HOW ARE WE GOING TO RIDE AN ELEVATOR WITH NO POWER?
BOXER DIDN'T WANT TO TELL HER WHAT HE REALLY HAD IN MIND.

OF COURSE, WHAT BOXER HAD IN MIND QUICKLY BECAME A MOOT POINT.
BOLLIX.
MISS MURAKAMI, YOU'RE GOING TO HAVE TO LEAVE YOUR BAGS BEHIND AND TRUST ME FOR THIS NEXT PART.
TRUST YOU? I DON'T EVEN KNOW... OH, NO.
HELL NO.
TELL ME YOU'VE DONE THIS BEFORE.
I'VE DONE THIS BEFORE.
BOXER HAD NEVER DONE THIS BEFORE.

OH, MY GOD, IS THAT... HIM OR...
...IT!?
DIDN'T YOU THINK IT WOULD BE A GOOD IDEA TO TELL ME FREAKIN' GODZILLA WAS ATTACKING?!
SPAK
SPAK
SPAK
SPAK
SPAK

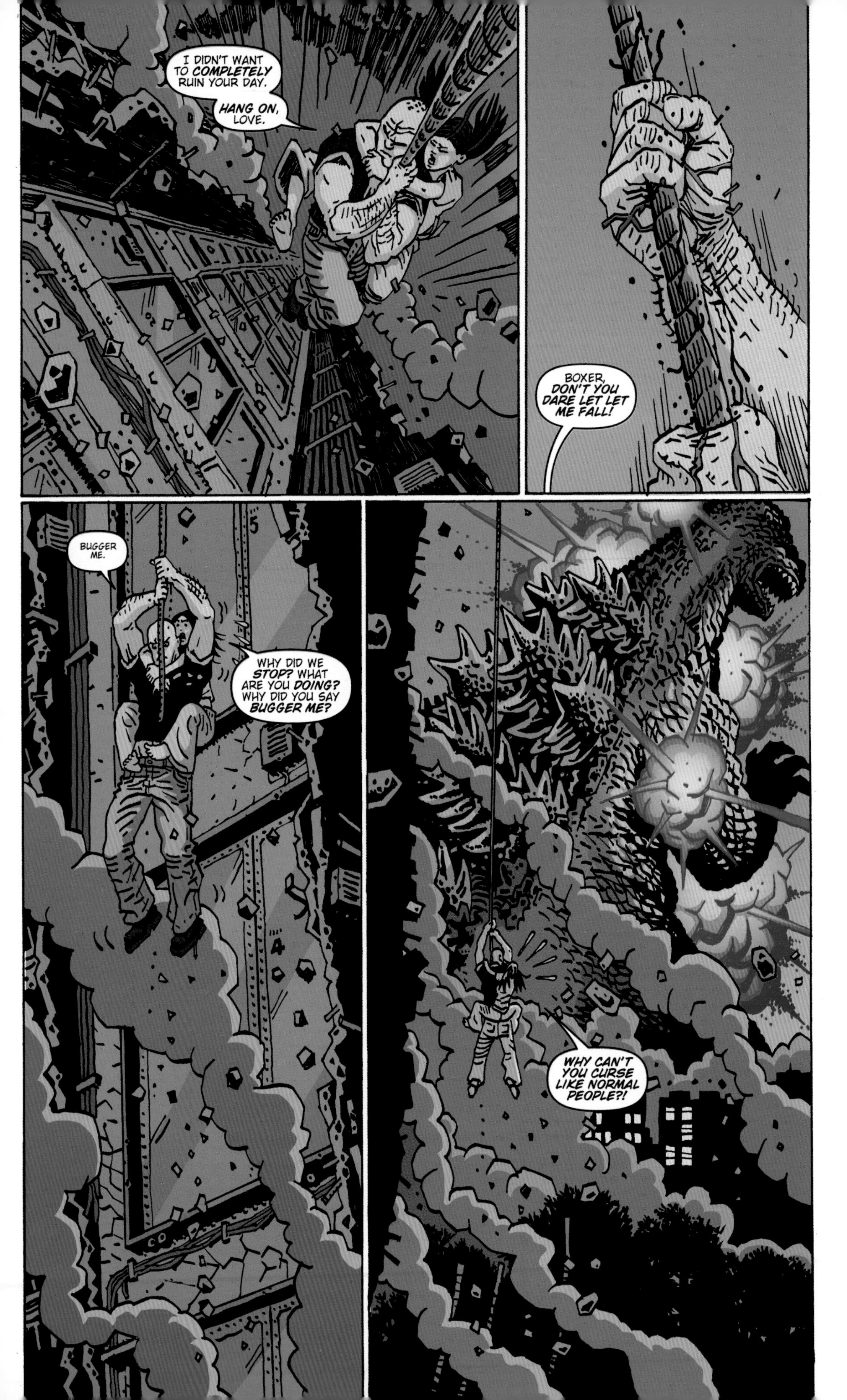
I DIDN'T WANT TO COMPLETELY RUIN YOUR DAY.
HANG ON, LOVE.
BOXER, DON'T YOU DARE LET LET ME FALL!
BUGGER ME.
WHY DID WE STOP? WHAT ARE YOU DOING? WHY DID YOU SAY BUGGER ME?
WHY CAN'T YOU CURSE LIKE NORMAL PEOPLE?!

HUH!

AAAAIIIIEEEEEEEEE!!!

KRAK
KRAK
KRAK
KRAK
KRAK
KRAK

BOXER!
KRAK
OOF!
WHUMP
YOU JUST...
...WE JUST...
TOLD YOU YOU COULD TRUST ME.

WHAT THE &$%* ARE YOU TWO DOING HERE? CLEAR THE AREA NOW!

TOO LITTLE, TOO LATE, YA STUPID #$@&. YA SHOULD'VE CLEARED EVERYONE HOURS AGO WHEN THIS BUGGER FIRST CRAWLED OUT OF HIS GRAVE!
WHERE'S THIS BILLION-DOLLAR EARLY ATTACK WARNING SYSTEM I KEEP READIN' ABOUT IN THE PAPERS?

THAT SYSTEM IS NOT QUITE... FULLY OPERATIONAL YET.

LOOK, BUDDY, GET YOUR DAUGHTER OUT OF THE CITY. AS FAST AS YOU CAN, ANY WAY YOU CAN.

YOU USED TO BE SOME BIG BAD SOLDIER, RIGHT? THOSE JERKS DON'T SEEM TO KNOW WHAT THEY'RE DOING. WHY DON'T YOU STAY AND HELP THEM?
LOOK, I CAN TAKE CARE OF MYSELF. MY MOM'S JUST ACROSS THE PARK THERE.

HEH. YOU WOULDN'T LAST TWO SECONDS WITHOUT ME.
BOXER...
...WHO THE HELL ARE THEY?

YOU BETTER TAKE YER LITTLE DATE THERE SOMEPLACE ELSE, MISTER. AND RIGHT QUICK.
WE HEARD ON THE RADIO THAT THE BIG GREY GECKO IS HEADED THIS WAY.

OY, WHAT ARE YA, A BUNCHA PAINTBALLERS? GET YER STUPID ARSES OUT OF HERE BEFORE YA GET SOMEONE KILLED.
LISTEN, BROTHER, YOU DON'T UNDERSTAND. THE GOVERNMENT'S CHALKING UP D.C. AS A TOTAL LOSS. GOVERNMENT'S ABOUT PROTECTIN' GOVERNMENT NOW, NOT ITS CITIZENS.

HEY, WHY DON'T YOU STAY? HELP DEFEND YOUR COUNTRY?
AIN'T MY COUNTRY, MATE.

DADDY! IT'S *HIM!*
SKREEEEEE-ONNNNNK!

NAIL HIS SCALY ASS!
BRAKKA BRAKKA B
BLAM
BLAM
BLAM
BL

BRAKKA
BRA
B
KKA
#$@% NO!

BREAKING
GODZILLA ATTACKS LOS ANGELES...
BEERS
ALES
YOU SHOULD HAVE BEEN HERE.
SHE DIED BECAUSE *YOU WEREN'T HERE.*

FOR THE FIRST TIME IN HIS VIOLENT LIFE, BOXER HAD FAILED.
HE CONSIDERED THIS UNFORGIVABLE.
NOW, THE LEAST HE COULD DO WAS BRING GWEN BACK TO HER MOTHER.
HUH?
SKREEEEE-ONNNNNK!
BOXER SAW THAT IT HAD FINALLY COME FOR HIM.

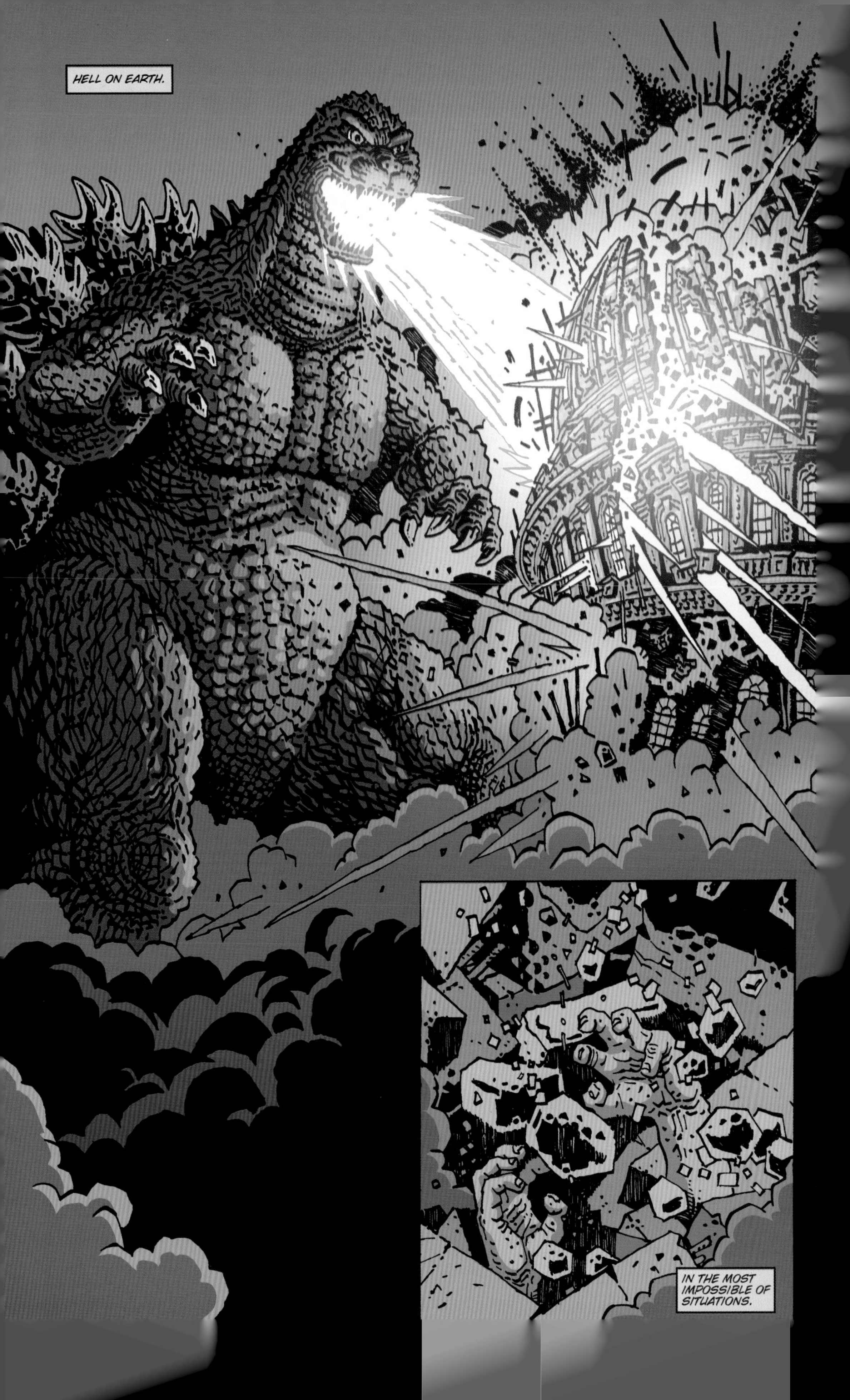
HELL ON EARTH.
IN THE MOST IMPOSSIBLE OF SITUATIONS.

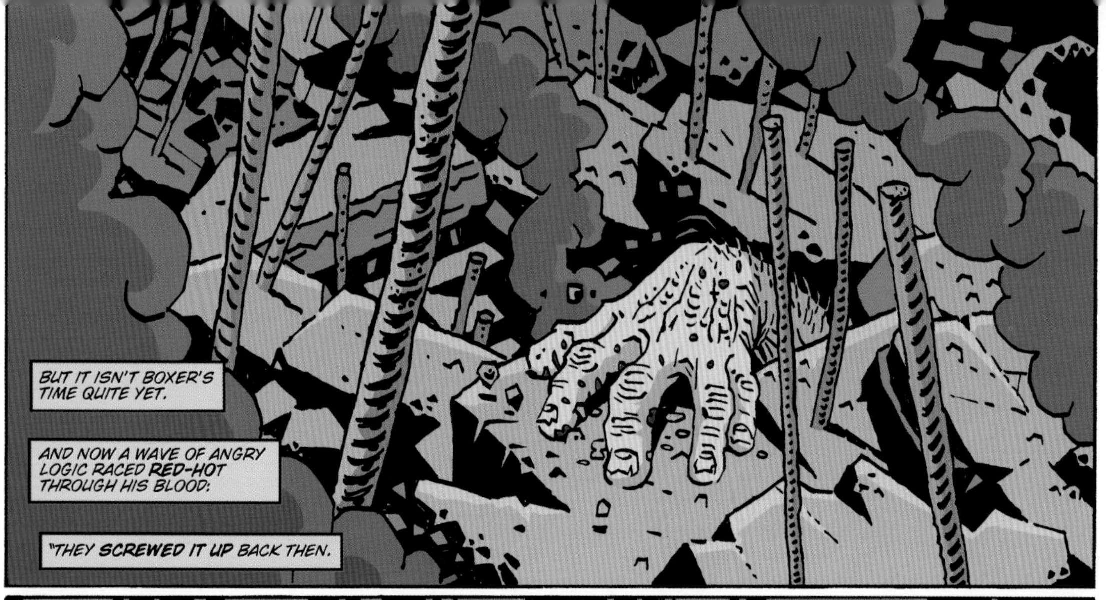
BUT IT ISN'T BOXER'S TIME QUITE YET.
AND NOW A WAVE OF ANGRY LOGIC RACED RED-HOT THROUGH HIS BLOOD:
"THEY SCREWED IT UP BACK THEN.

"THEY'RE SCREWING IT UP NOW.

"THEY'RE GOING TO KEEP SCREWING AROUND WITH THE GIANT MONSTERS, AND KEEP GETTING SCREWED.

"THAT IS, UNLESS SOMEONE TAKES CARE OF THEM ONCE AND FOR ALL."

05:57
WHICH IS WHEN HE CALLED AN OLD FRIEND.
OY. URV.
WHATCHA DOIN' THIS WEEKEND?

ART BY ZACH HOWARD
COLORS BY NELSON DANIEL

PITTSBURGH, PENNSYLVANIA
People, you are never gonna believe the photo I just got. Stay tuned...
Sorry! The server is busy. Try posting your message again later.
Okay, ladies and gents, check this out, live from Pittsburgh, the one and only

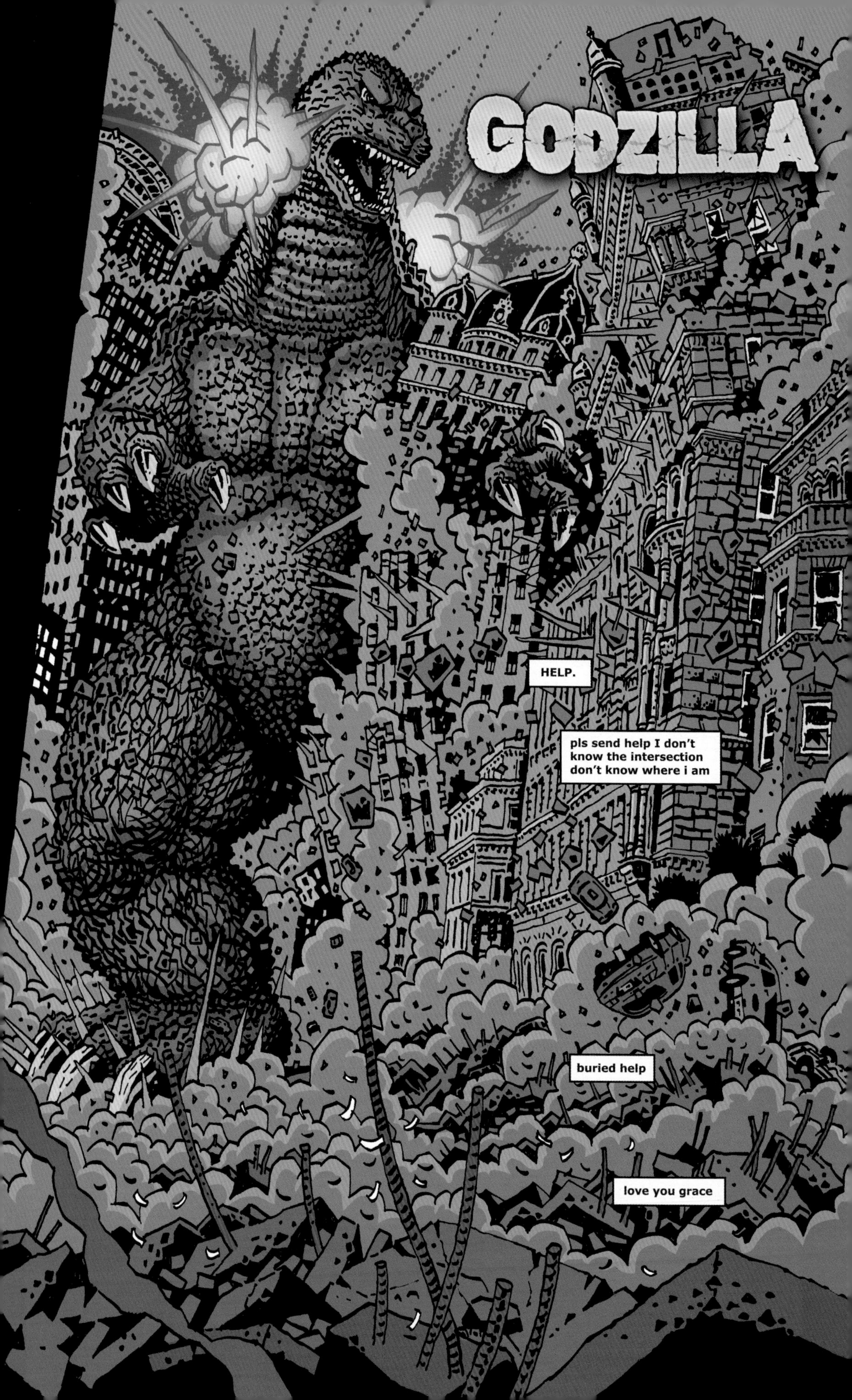
GODZILLA
HELP.
pls send help I don't
know the intersection
don't know where i am
buried help
love you grace

NOGALES, ARIZONA
ON THE U.S.-MEXICO BORDER
@Dirk_Hagen Get your ass over to Memorial Park... word is that thing just invaded the homeland!
@Dirk_Hagen Tell the guys to lock and load so we can send this creepy crawler back to Mexico.
U.S. BORDER PATROL
U.S. BORDER PATROL
BORDER PATROL
@LexiUSA Where are u?
@LexiUSA cmon honey, where are you? Talk to me.

EDINBURGH, SCOTLAND
So this is the way the world ends.
Not with a bang. Or a whimper, as Eliot claimed.
But with a tweet.
Love and luck to you all.

PART TWO:

GIANT
MONSTERS
ARE THE
DISEASE

MEET THE CURE...

WOT?

YOU HAVE NO PLAN? SO LET ME GET THIS STRAIGHT, BOXER.
YOU HAD ME STEAL ALL OF THIS GEAR, HIJACK A CHOPPER, FLY HALFWAY AROUND THE WORLD... AND YET YOU HAVE NO PLAN?!

NEED TO SEE THE SITUATION ON THE GROUND FIRST.
YOU KNOW, I CAN PRETTY MUCH SEE THE GROUND FROM HERE.

"AND I MIGHT CHARACTERIZE THE SITUATION AS... HOPELESSLY SCREWED."

NO OFFENSE, MAN, SHE HAS A POINT. WHY THE HELL DID WE FLY ALL THE WAY TO SCOTLAND? THERE ARE PLENTY OF THESE THINGS EVERYWHERE.
LIKE THAT EVIL SPIDER THING WHO KILLED MY HUSBAND BACK IN MEXICO.
OVER THE PAST FEW DAYS, FOR REASONS UNKNOWN, THE GIANT MONSTERS HAD RISEN UP ONCE AGAIN ALL OVER THE WORLD.

AND BOXER, AFTER SUFFERING TWO INTENSELY PERSONAL LOSSES, DECIDED TO RISE UP AGAINST THEM.

TO PUT AN END TO THEM.

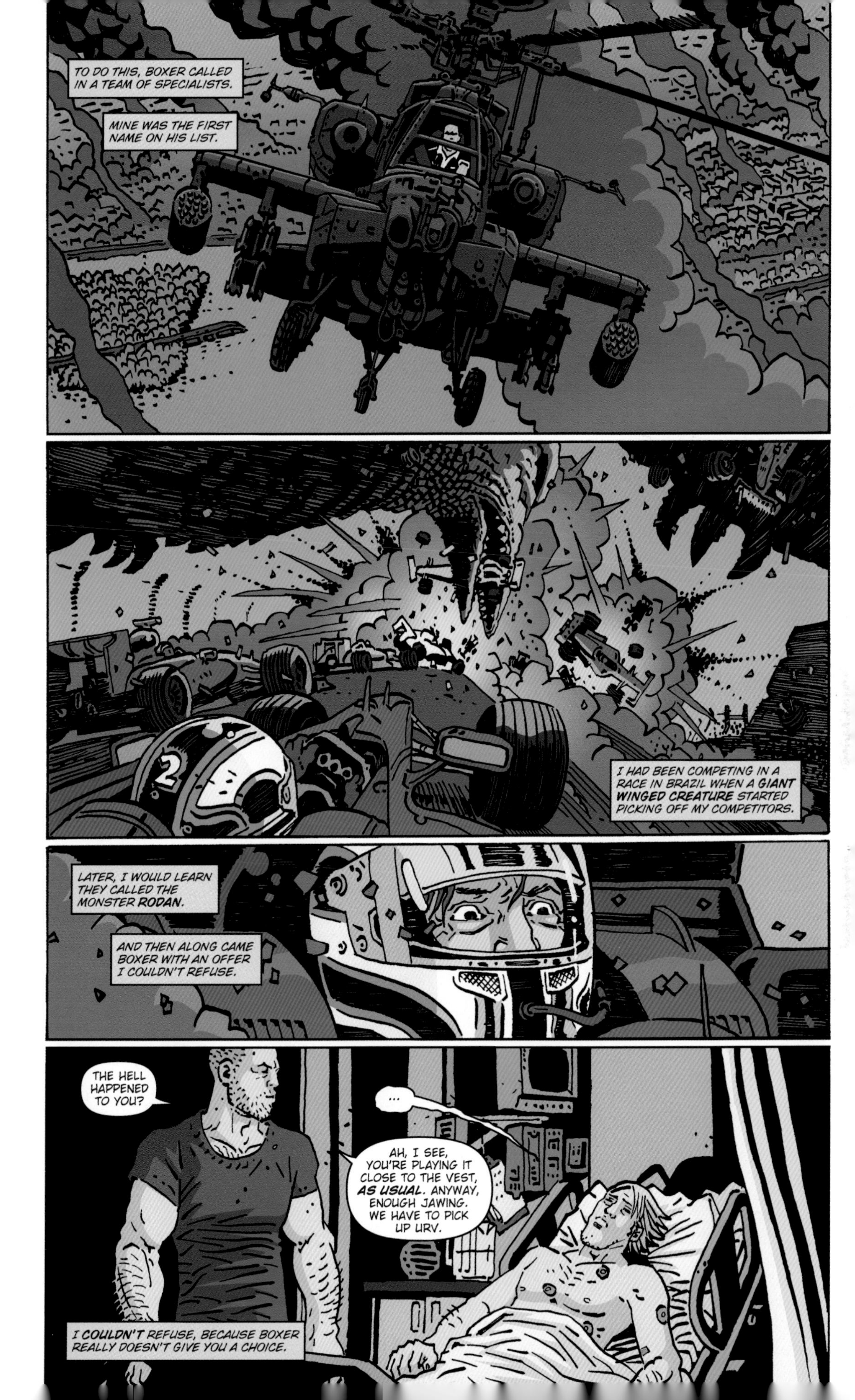
TO DO THIS, BOXER CALLED IN A TEAM OF SPECIALISTS.
MINE WAS THE FIRST NAME ON HIS LIST.
I HAD BEEN COMPETING IN A RACE IN BRAZIL WHEN A GIANT WINGED CREATURE STARTED PICKING OFF MY COMPETITORS.
LATER, I WOULD LEARN THEY CALLED THE MONSTER RODAN.
AND THEN ALONG CAME BOXER WITH AN OFFER I COULDN'T REFUSE.
THE HELL HAPPENED TO YOU?
...
AH, I SEE, YOU'RE PLAYING IT CLOSE TO THE VEST, AS USUAL. ANYWAY, ENOUGH JAWING. WE HAVE TO PICK UP URV.
I COULDN'T REFUSE, BECAUSE BOXER REALLY DOESN'T GIVE YOU A CHOICE.

URV, THOUGH, WAS JUST AS BLOOD CRAZY AS BOXER. HIS ENTIRE FAMILY, INCLUDING HIS GROOM-TO-BE, HAD BEEN KILLED BY A CREATURE THEY CALLED KUMONGA. HE WANTED REVENGE.
BROTHER, WAS I GLAD TO HEAR YOUR VOICE.
ANYWAY, I GOT A BEAT ON THAT UNHOLY MONSTER UP IN ARIZONA, AND—
NOT YET, MATE. THERE'S ONE MORE MEMBER OF THE TEAM TO PICK UP, AND ANOTHER TARGET I HAVE IN MIND.
WHAT? WE'RE RIGHT HERE! I THOUGHT YOU SAID YOU WANTED TO DESTROY THESE THINGS!
SORRY, BROTHER, BUT WE'VE GOT TO DO IT MY WAY. OTHERWISE THE ENTIRE PLAN FALLS APART.
WHO'S THIS? ANOTHER ONE OF YOUR LOST BOYS FROM MISSIONS PAST?
URV, HARRISON. HARRISON'S THE DRIVER. HE'S ALSO MUTE.
...
HARRISON, URV. URV'S A SWISH AND ONE HELL OF AN EXPLOSIVES MAN.
WE ALL CAUGHT UP NOW? BECAUSE WE NEED TO PICK UP ONE OF MY EXES IN SOUTH KOREA IN... OH, RIGHT ABOUT NOW.
"OTHERWISE, WE DON'T HAVE A PRAYER AGAINST THESE THINGS."

BOXER'S EX TURNED OUT TO BE **CLAIRE PLANGMAN**, AN ARMY SCIENTIST STATIONED AT YONGSAN GARRISON.
SHE WAS THE LAST PERSON LEFT ALIVE ON THE BASE.

Creeeeeeeeeee

OY! **EASY THERE**, SHOTGUN SALLY.

SO... WHERE IS IT?

OOOH THAT'S IT, INNIT?

WHAT IS THAT THING?
I'LL LET CLAIRE EXPLAIN THE SCIENTIFIC BITS AND BOBS TO YOU ON THE CHOPPER, BUT IT'S HOW WE'RE GOING TO DESTROY THESE OVERSIZED, UGLY B—
BOOM
GEE, BOXER, NO WORRIES, I'M FINE. I'VE ONLY BEEN HOLED UP IN THIS STINKING SUPPLY DEPOT WITH NO FOOD OR WATER FOR TWO DAYS STRAIGHT BECAUSE YOU TOLD ME YOU'D BE RIGHT OVER...
HEY, IT'S A LITTLE NUTS OUT THERE, IN CASE YOU HAVEN'T NOTICED.
YOU'VE KEPT ME WAITING WAYYY TOO MANY TIMES FOR IT TO HAPPEN AGAIN.
I'LL APOLOGIZE ON THE CHOPPER.
I DIDN'T HEAR A CHOPPER LAND.
"RIGHT. WE NEED TO STEAL ONE. GOT ANY LEFT ON BASE?
"ALSO GOING TO NEED A LIGHT ARMORED VEHICLE AND ENOUGH C-4 TO TAKE DOWN KILIMANJARO. BOYS, HELP ME PULL THIS THING OUT, WILLYA?"

EDINBURGH. NOW.
THE CLOCK TOWER OVER WAVERLY STATION HAD TOLD THE TIME TO COUNTLESS CITY RESIDENTS FOR WELL OVER A CENTURY.
11:12 A.M., THE LAST TIME IT WOULD EVER TELL.
THANKS TO A MONSTER THEY CALLED ANGUIRUS.
WORD WAS SPREADING QUICK THROUGHOUT THE BATTERED CITY: EDINBURGH WAS CONSIDERED A TOTAL LOSS, BEYOND SAVING.
City Sightseeing
Edinburgh

UNTIL, OF COURSE, WE SHOWED UP.

MY GOD... BOXER? IS THAT YOU?
BANKS

HOW LONG'S IT BEEN, MATE? THE BOYS ARE GOING TO BE THRILLED TO SEE YOU. WE'VE BEEN TAKING A SERIOUS BEATING—

ULK

NO OFFENSE, MATE, BUT I DON'T NEED A SPEECH, I NEED SOMEONE WITH REAL AUTHORITY.
ONE OF YOU BOYS GET ME PERMANENT SECRETARY RAPHAEL WENT ON A FIELD PHONE.

BOXER? YOU PICKED AN AWFULLY BAD TIME TO PLAY CATCH-UP. WE JUST LOST EDINBURGH, AND—

YOU HAVEN'T LOST IT YET. ME AND MY MATES, WE'RE GONNA TAKE CARE OF YOUR MONSTER PROBLEM.
OH REALLY. AND HOW DO YOU PROPOSE TO DO THAT?
PAY US SEVEN BILLION POUNDS AND YOU'LL FIND OUT.

SEVEN WHAT? ARE YOU INSANE?
FINE, YEAH, I'M BONKERS. BUT YOU'VE GOT THE CASH AND THE AUTHORITY TO MAKE THIS DEAL. WE FAIL TO TAKE DOWN THIS SPIKED BASTARD, YOU PAY NOTHING.

"DO YOU REALLY WANT TO BE THE GUY WHO TURNED US DOWN WHEN WE STOP ANOTHER ONE OF THESE MONSTERS IN ANOTHER CITY?"

LET'S GET THE PILL BUG'S ATTENTION.
GOT A LITTLE SOMETHING FOR HIM, URV?
SURE DO.
JUST A LITTLE SOMETHING TO CLEAR OUT ANGUIRUS' SINUSES.
VROOOOOOOM
EEEYAAA WAAAHHH

YOU CERTAINLY GOT HIS ATTENTION, URV.
SCREEE
BUS LANE
OY, HARRISON! *MOVE MOVE MOVE!*
EEEYAAA WAAAHHH
VROOOM
WHOAH!

AND YOUR HANDS JUST SO HAPPENED TO GO *THERE.*
Lothian

SLAM
Hardie
IN YOUR DREAMS.
YOU TWO EVER GONNA *STOP* BICKERING?
...!!!

OKAY, WE GOT THE BUGGER INTERESTED. WE NEED TO GET BEHIND THE CASTLE, DROP OFF URV, THEN SWING AROUND TO HIGH STREET.
OH, SO NOW YOU'VE GOT A PLAN?
AS LONG AS THIS GIZMO OF YOURS WORKS, YEAH, I'VE GOT A PLAN.
YOU KNOW WHAT TO DO AT THE CASTLE, RIGHT?
JUST GET ME THERE AND I'LL TAKE CARE OF THE REST.
SSSSSKREEEEEEEEE
GUH!
EEEEEEEEE

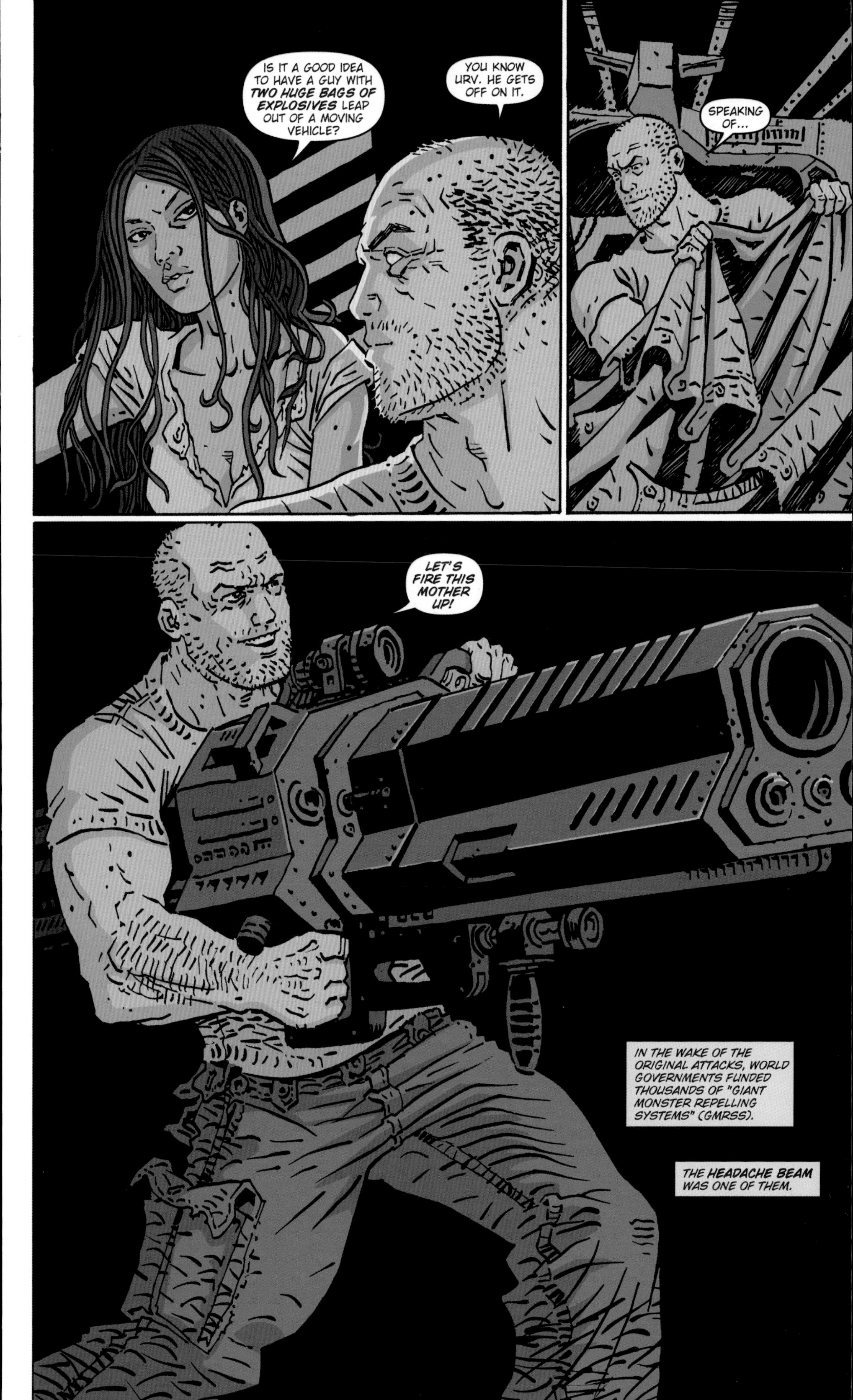
IS IT A GOOD IDEA TO HAVE A GUY WITH TWO HUGE BAGS OF EXPLOSIVES LEAP OUT OF A MOVING VEHICLE?
YOU KNOW URV. HE GETS OFF ON IT.
SPEAKING OF...
LET'S FIRE THIS MOTHER UP!
IN THE WAKE OF THE ORIGINAL ATTACKS, WORLD GOVERNMENTS FUNDED THOUSANDS OF "GIANT MONSTER REPELLING SYSTEMS" (GMRSS).
THE HEADACHE BEAM WAS ONE OF THEM.

CLAIRE DESIGNED IT TO ADDLE THE BRAINS OF GIANT MONSTERS. NOBODY BELIEVED IT COULD WORK.
NOBODY BUT ITS INVENTOR, CLAIRE PLANGMAN.
OKAY, IT'S ONLINE.
beep beep beep

SO HERE'S THE PLAN, LOVE: WE'RE GONNA GIVE THE BUGGER A HEADACHE, STEER 'EM UP HIGH STREET, THEN LET URV HANDLE THE REST.

FOR THIS TO WORK, HARRISON, I'LL NEED YOU TO DRIVE AS CLOSE AS YOU CAN TO THE MONSTER, AND THEN WE'LL—

THROOOOM

KRESHHH
THAT LOUSY PILL BUG...
CRONK

GUESS IT WOULD BE TOO MUCH TO ASSUME YOU HAD A BACK-UP PLAN, EH, BOXER?

ART BY MATT FRANK

ART BY ZACH HOWARD
COLORS BY NELSON DANIEL

EDINBURGH, SCOTLAND
WHERE THE HELL DO I EVEN BEGIN TO RECAP THIS?
DO I START WITH THE FACT THAT OUR VAN WAS JUST HEADBUTTED... TWICE... BY A GIANT HORNED MONSTER?
OR THAT THE ONLY WEAPON THAT COULD MAYBE STOP IT JUST SNAPPED IN HALF?
DON'T YOU REMEMBER WHERE THE DAMNED WIRES GO? YOU DESIGNED THE BLOODY THING!
YOU DIDN'T KNOW TO MAKE IT SHATTERPROOF, DIDJA?
SHUT UP! I KNOW WHAT I'M DOING.

NO. I KNOW WHERE TO BEGIN:
WE WERE IN EDINBURGH, ABOUT TO BE CRUSHED TO DEATH BY A GIANT MONSTER KNOWN AS ANGUIRUS. AND I WAS ASKED TO DO THE IMPOSSIBLE.
OY! HARRISON!
WE NEED YOU TO BUY US A LITTLE TIME, BOYO!

PART THREE:
THIS TIME
IT'S PERSONAL
HOT-WIRED AND ROLLING WITHIN 4 SECONDS. A NEW PERSONAL BEST.
ZZZT
HONK HONKHONK
HONK
VROOOooM
CLAIRE.
YOU'RE GONNA WANT TO JUST LET YOUR BODY ROLL WITH IT.
ROLL WITH—

—WHAT?!
WHUMP
VRRRRMMMMMMM
WHOOOOOSH

OHMYGOD OHMYGODOH MYGOD—
SSCCRRREEEEEEeeeee
FOCUS, PLANGMAN! WE NEED THIS WEAPON OPERATIONAL.
FOCUS. RIGHT...
...FOCUS ON THE HOOD OF A SPEEDING CAR...
OY!
GET AS CLOSE AS YOU CAN TO THAT THING. LET'S NOT KEEP URV WAITING.
OKAY! IT SHOULD WORK NOW!
'BOUT BLOODY TIME.

I REMEMBER THINKING: PLEASE PLEASE PLEASE LET THIS WORK.
SCREEEEEEEEEE
HERE'S ONE BETWEEN YER EYES, PILL BUG.
HUZZZZZUUUMMM

NO OFFENSE TO CLAIRE... BUT I WAS KINDA SURPRISED WHEN IT **DID** WORK.
EEEYAAWAAHHH
YES.
THAT'S RIGHT, YOU BASTARD.
I HOPE YOU'RE HAVING THE **WORST HANGOVER** OF YER HORNY LIFE.

AS CLAIRE EXPLAINED ON THE PLANE, HER SO-CALLED HEADACHE BEAM WASN'T ABLE TO INFLICT ANY REAL DAMAGE ON A GIANT MONSTER.
NO LIQUEFYING HIS BRAIN, NO SHORT-CIRCUITING HIS NERVOUS SYSTEM.
INSTEAD, THE BEAM JUST ANNOYS THE LIVING CRAP OUT OF IT.
NUDGING IT TO A PLACE OF OUR CHOOSING.

THROOM
NOW!
THREE...
"TWO..."
INTERESTING THING ABOUT EDINBURGH'S LANDMARK CASTLE.

"DONE."
IT JUST SO HAPPENED TO BE BUILT OVER AN EXTINCT VOLCANO.
BOOOM

I COULD HARDLY BELIEVE IT.
I CAN'T *BELIEVE IT*.
-KOFF KOFF- ME, NEITHER.
BELIEVE IT!
LADY AND GENTLEMEN... WE ARE IN *BUSINESS*.

ATTENTION WAS BOXER TOOK OF THE SPOTLIGHT INTENTIONS KNOWN.
YEAH, WE'LL KEEP TAKING THESE ABOMINATIONS DOWN, BUT NOT FOR FREE.
WE WANT SEVEN BILLION A MONSTER.
DID YOU SAY SEVEN BILLION, SIR? HOW DID YOU COME UP WITH THAT FIGURE?
EH, THAT'S ONLY A BUCK FOR EVERY LIVING PERSON ON EARTH.
A BARGAIN, REALLY.
LIVE
BED US THE KILL CREW.
NEWS 24
AND WITH BILLIONS OF COLLECTIVE ACCOUNTS, WE ON OUR FIRST WORLD TOUR
PLANET EARTH'S SAVIORS... OR EXTORTIONISTS?

TAOS, NEW MEXICO
BEEN WAITING FOR THIS MOMENT.
FANTASIZING ABOUT IT. OH MAN, LIKE YOU WOULDN'T BELIEVE.
I JUST WISH YOU COULD UNDERSTAND MY WORDS. WISH YOU COULD HAVE SOME INKLING OF THE HURT AND RAGE INSIDE MY HEART.
BUT YOU HAVE NO IDEA, DO YOU?
SCRAPE
SCRAPE
SCRAPE
URV, MATE... YOU ABOUT DONE?
NOT TRYIN' TA RUSH YOU OR ANYTHING, BUT...

YEAH. I'M DONE.
CLICK
CHOOM
CHOOM
CHOOM
CHOOM
CHOOM
URV WOULD NEVER ADMIT AS MUCH...
...BUT I GOT THE FEELING THAT PUNISHING KUMONGA DIDN'T DO A THING TO EASE THE ACHE IN HIS SOUL.

SAO PAULO, BRAZIL
NOW ME, ON THE OTHER HAND...
I'LL CONFESS THAT I ENJOYED SEEING THAT BIG BIRD SUFFER.
HARRISON, YOU BOLLIX! TURN RIGHT! WE NEED TO HERD THIS FLAPPIN' BASTARD DOWN THE AVENIDA DA LIBERDADE!
RODAN HAD CERTAINLY CAUSED ME ENOUGH PAIN.
SKRAAAAAAAAA
KRESSHHHH
OH, NO.

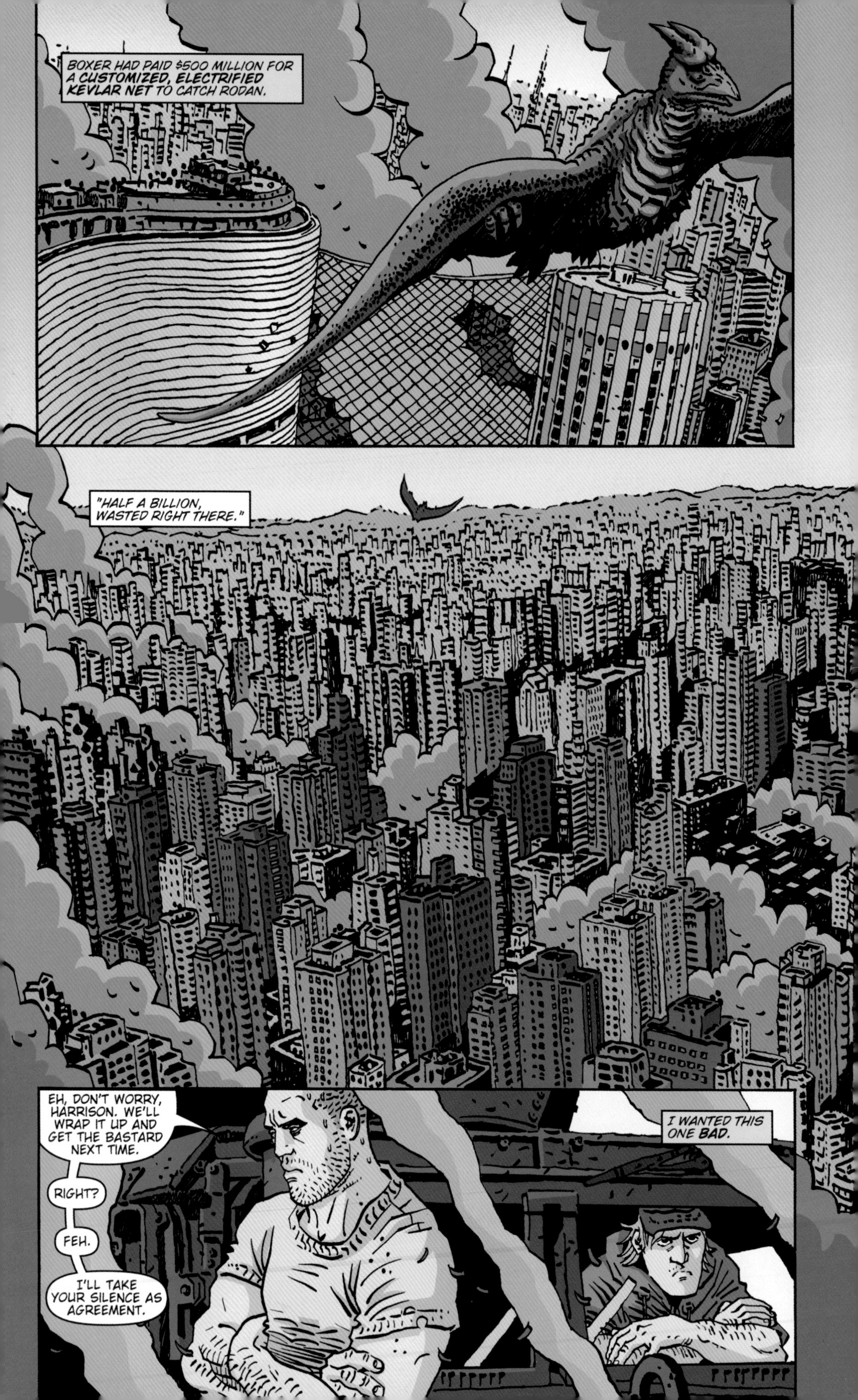
BOXER HAD PAID $500 MILLION FOR A CUSTOMIZED, ELECTRIFIED KEVLAR NET TO CATCH RODAN.
"HALF A BILLION, WASTED RIGHT THERE."
EH, DON'T WORRY, HARRISON. WE'LL WRAP IT UP AND GET THE BASTARD NEXT TIME.
I WANTED THIS ONE BAD.
RIGHT?
FEH.
I'LL TAKE YOUR SILENCE AS AGREEMENT.

YONGSANG GARRISON, SEOUL, SOUTH KOREA
ALMOST AS BAD AS CLAIRE WANTED TO HURT BATTRA.
THE GIANT FLYING MONSTER SLAUGHTERED MANY OF HER COLLEAGUES.
SHE HADN'T BEEN ABLE TO USE THE HEADACHE BEAM ON IT BECAUSE IT WAS TOO HEAVY FOR HER TO LIFT OR EVEN MOVE.
A DESIGN PROBLEM SHE'S SINCE LICKED.
WE READY FOR ANOTHER GO?
LET'S DO IT.
HAPPY FOURTH OF JULY, CLAIRE.
HUZZZUMMMMM
HUZZZUMMMMM
HUZZZUMM
HUZZZUMM
HZZZZZZZ
HUZZZZUMMM
HUZZZZZZZZZ
HUUUZZZZZZZ
AND THIS TIME...

...THE NET CAME IN HANDY.
ZZZZZZZZZZZZZ

ZAP

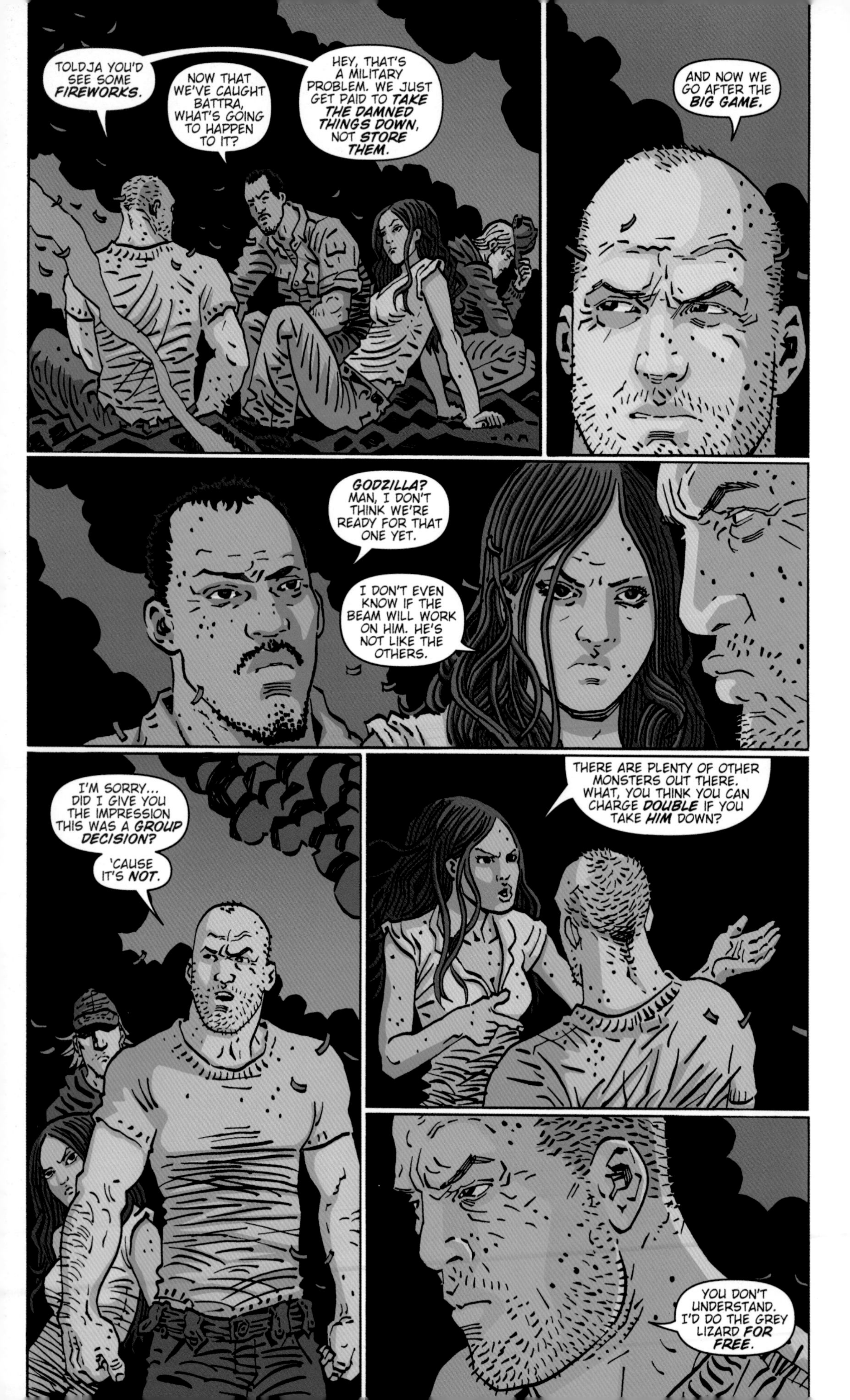
TOLDJA YOU'D SEE SOME FIREWORKS.
NOW THAT WE'VE CAUGHT BATTRA, WHAT'S GOING TO HAPPEN TO IT?
HEY, THAT'S A MILITARY PROBLEM. WE JUST GET PAID TO TAKE THE DAMNED THINGS DOWN, NOT STORE THEM.
AND NOW WE GO AFTER THE BIG GAME.
GODZILLA? MAN, I DON'T THINK WE'RE READY FOR THAT ONE YET.
I DON'T EVEN KNOW IF THE BEAM WILL WORK ON HIM. HE'S NOT LIKE THE OTHERS.
I'M SORRY... DID I GIVE YOU THE IMPRESSION THIS WAS A GROUP DECISION?
'CAUSE IT'S NOT.
THERE ARE PLENTY OF OTHER MONSTERS OUT THERE. WHAT, YOU THINK YOU CAN CHARGE DOUBLE IF YOU TAKE HIM DOWN?
YOU DON'T UNDERSTAND. I'D DO THE GREY LIZARD FOR FREE.

ST. LOUIS, MISSOURI
BOXER'S DAUGHTER DIED DURING GODZILLA'S L.A. RAMPAGE TWO YEARS AGO. BOXER HAD BEEN ON A JOB IN LONDON, AND BLAMED HIMSELF FOR NOT BEING HOME TO PROTECT HER.
NOT TOO LONG AGO, A GIRL UNDER BOXER'S CARE PERISHED DURING THE MOST RECENT ATTACK.
SAFE TO SAY... BOXER TOOK GODZILLA EXTREMELY PERSONAL.
BUT AS IT TURNED OUT, REVENGE WOULD HAVE TO WAIT.
YO, WE'VE GOT WORD OF SOMETHING MAULING THE HELL OUT OF TOKYO.
THAT'S A LOT CLOSER THAN MISSOURI.
GODDAMN IT.

TOKYO, JAPAN
"LET'S GO, THEN."
WHAT DO WE GOT?
NEWS IS REPORTING AN AMPHIBIOUS DINOSAUR. APPARENTLY ITS FAN-LIKE TAIL CAN CREATE HUGE WAVES OF...
WHOAH!
THE HELL WAS THAT, HARRISON?
THAT'S EXACTLY WHAT IT WAS.

HELL.

ART BY MATT FRANK

ART BY ZACH HOWARD
COLORS BY NELSON DANIEL

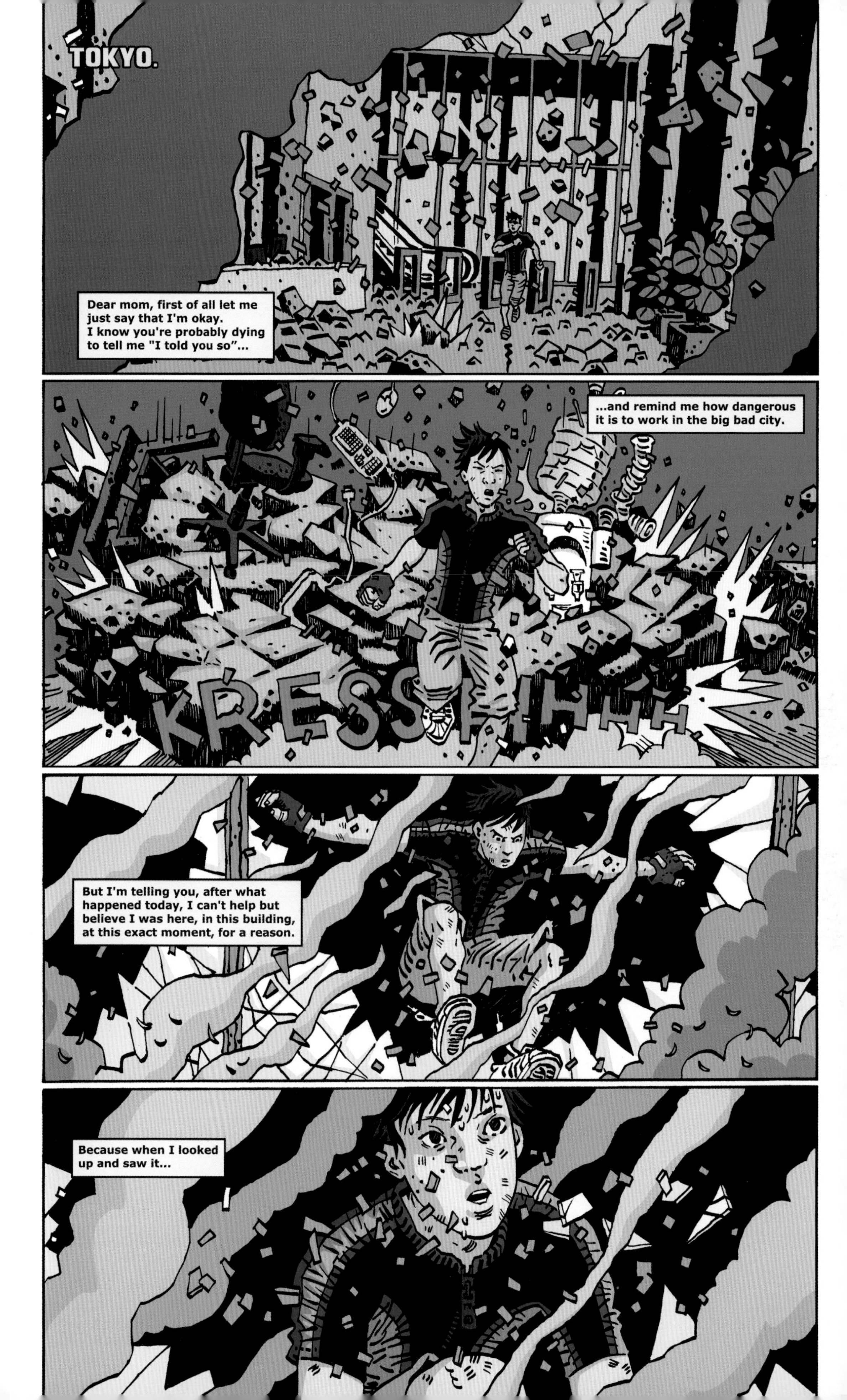

TOKYO.
Dear mom, first of all let me just say that I'm okay. I know you're probably dying to tell me "I told you so"...
...and remind me how dangerous it is to work in the big bad city.
KRESSHHHH
But I'm telling you, after what happened today, I can't help but believe I was here, in this building, at this exact moment, for a reason.
Because when I looked up and saw it...

went back
s a kid...
tally obsessed
osaurs.
ately thought
crazy British
know, the one
lying around
l these monsters?
Well, mom, don't
freak out...
...but I want to see
if he'd ever consider
hiring an intern.

5,000 FEET ABOVE TOKYO.
WE WERE ON OUR WAY TO TOKYO TO DEAL WITH ONE GIANT MONSTER WHEN A SECOND ONE SHOWED UP.
IF I DIDN'T KNOW BETTER, I'D SWEAR RODAN WAS MAKING THIS PERSONAL.
OY.
WE MUSTA REALLY GOTTEN THIS BIG BIRD'S KNICKERS IN A TWIST.
BOXER, WILL YOU COME ON!
AND EVEN THOUGH THE EXPERTS SAY THE GIANT MONSTERS DON'T GIVE US ANY MORE THOUGHT THAN WE GIVE INSECTS... I DON'T KNOW.
SKRAAAAAAAA
IT SURE AS HELL FELT PERSONAL.

YOU DON'T ASSIGN HIM A GIANT MONSTER

YOU JUST TURN HIM LOOSE

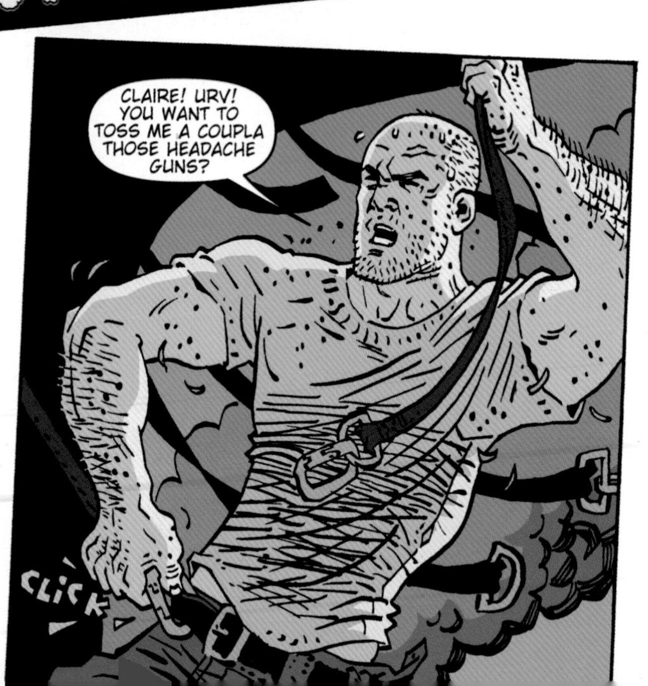

SKRAAAAA
GONNA GIVE YOU THE **WORST HANGOVER** YOU'VE EVER EXPERIENCED, MY NON-FEATHERED FRIEND.

SKRAAAAAAAAAAAAAA

DIDJA **SEE THAT**, CLAIRE? YOU NEED TO MAKE A **DOUBLE-BARRELED** VERSION OF THIS HEAD—
BOXER-LOOK-OUT!

FFWOOOOOOOM
KRESSSHHHHHHH

KRAK-SSHKK
BOLLIX.
I'M RIGHT BACK WHERE I STARTED.

OH, MAN.
WE'VE NEVER HAD TO DEAL WITH **TWO OF THESE THINGS** BEFORE.

WELL, BOXER, THERE GOES YOUR PLAN. *AGAIN.*

NEW PLAN THEN.
WE FORCE THE FLAPPY ONE...
...TO FIGHT THAT 'UN.
"THEN WHEN THEY'RE ALL TUCKERED OUT, WE TAKE 'EM BOTH DOWN."
CLAIRE, GRAB US TWO FUNCTIONAL HEADACHE GIZMOS. URV, PREPARE YOUR EXPLOSIVES AS PLANNED. HARRISON, GATHER UP AS MANY PARACHUTES AS YOU CAN FIND.
PARACHUTES? THERE'S NO WAY I'M JUMPING OUT OF—
DID I SAY "CLAIRE, GATHER UP THE PARACHUTES?" NO, I SAID "HARRISON, GATHER UP THE PARACHUTES." LET'S STAY FOCUSED, TEAM.
I WAS WITH CLAIRE. NO WAY WAS I JUMPING OUT OF THIS CHOPPER.

BUT AS IT TURNED OUT BOXER HAD SOMETHING QUITE DIFFERENT IN MIND.
I'VE GOT FLAPPY, YOU TAKE DINO OVER THERE.
HZZZZZZ
ZZZZZZZZZZ
"I DON'T THINK THE BEAM IS HAVING ANY EFFECT ON THE DINOSAUR. DAMNIT, BOXER, I WARNED YOU ABOUT THE BIOLOGICAL DIFFERENCES BETWEEN—"
"NO WORRIES, CLAIRE. I'LL TAKE CARE OF IT FROM MY END."
SKRAAAAA
FLAP
FLAP
THAT'S IT... WATCH THE BIRDIE, WATCH THE BIRDIE...
HUZZZZZ ZZZZZ

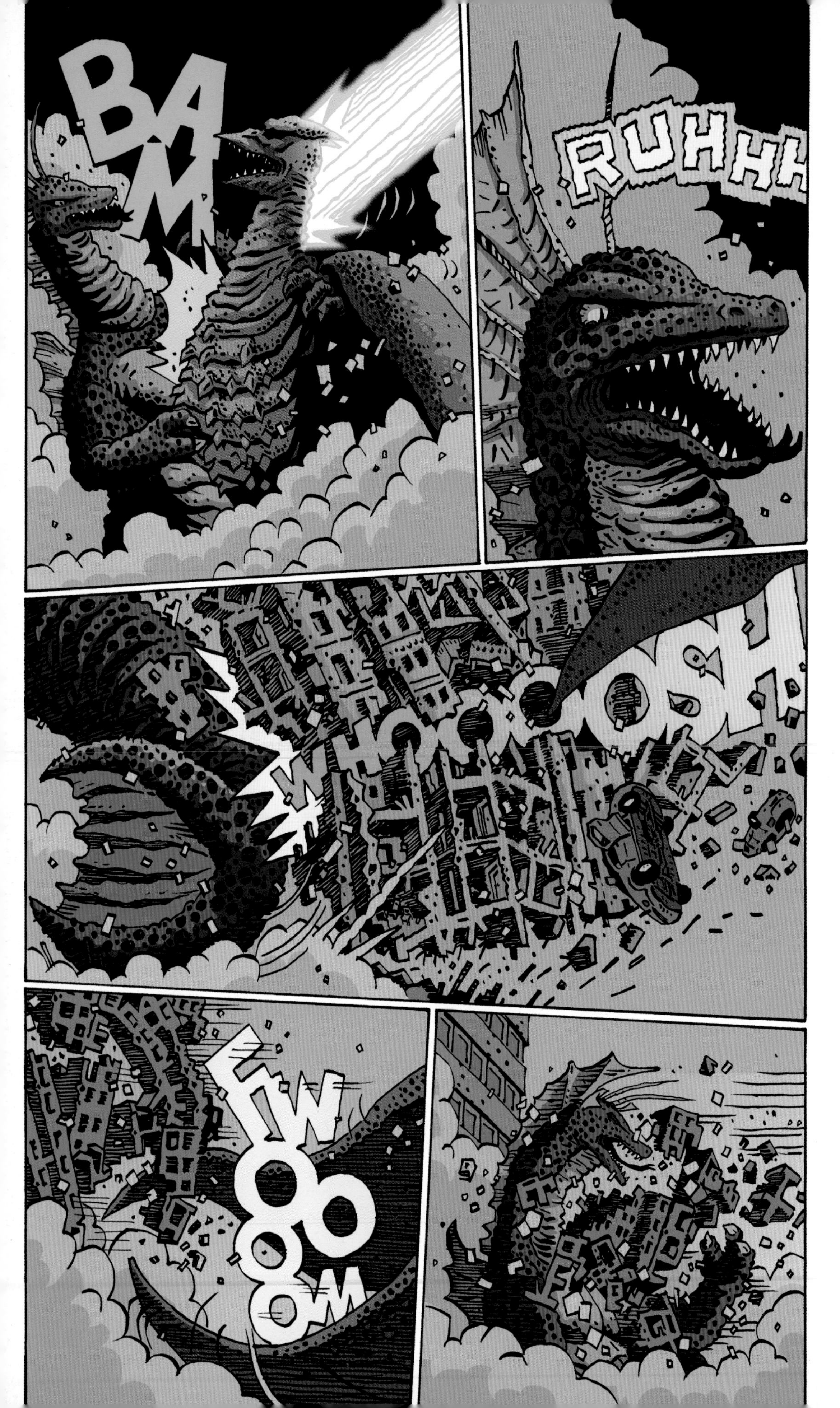
BAM
RUHHH
WHOOOOSH!
FWOOOOM

SSKRRRRUUUUTCH
RRUH-RUH-
REEEONK
DON'T RUSH ME.
WE READY YET?
SLAMM

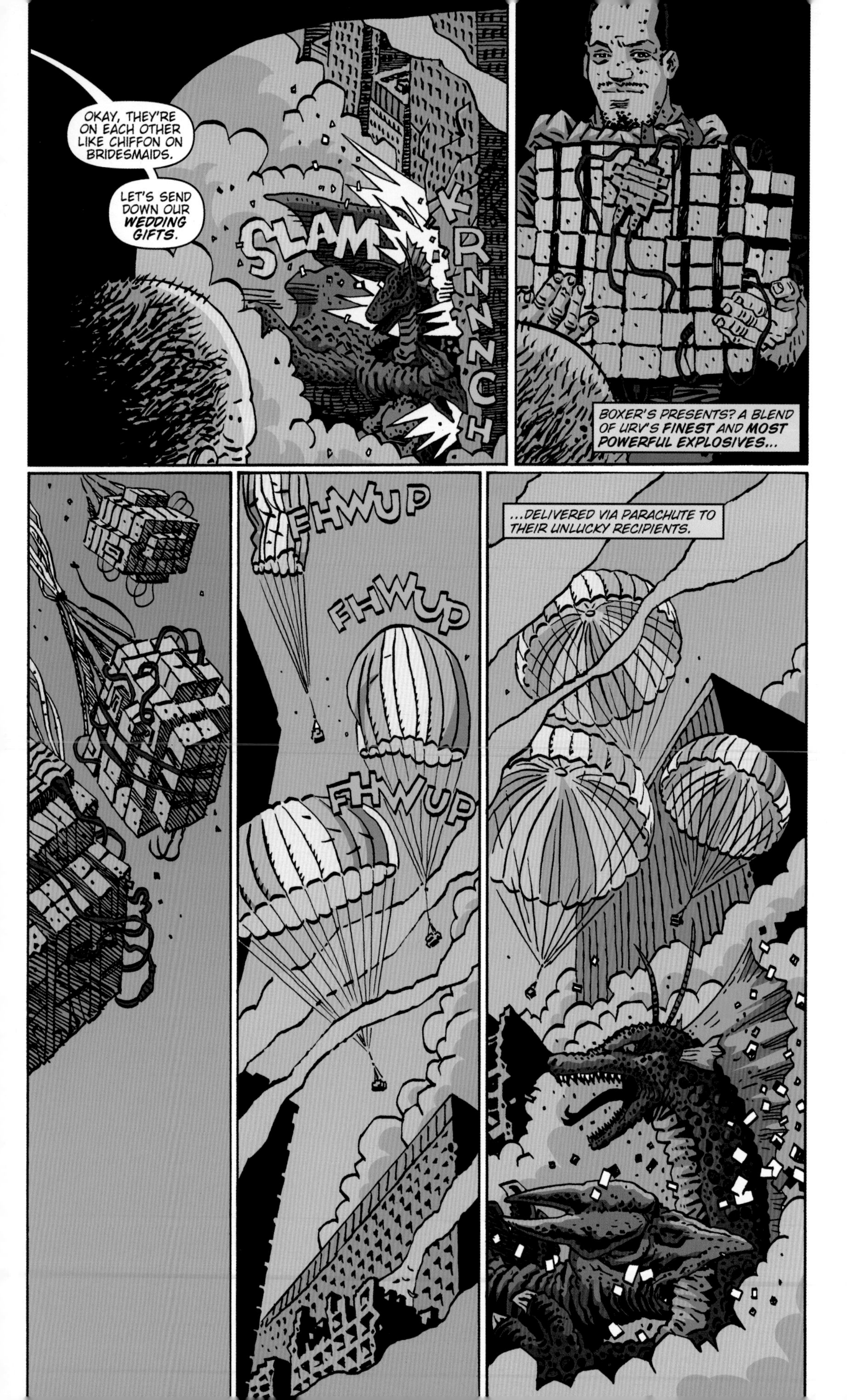
OKAY, THEY'RE ON EACH OTHER LIKE CHIFFON ON BRIDESMAIDS.
LET'S SEND DOWN OUR WEDDING GIFTS.
SLAM
KRNNNCH
BOXER'S PRESENTS? A BLEND OF URV'S FINEST AND MOST POWERFUL EXPLOSIVES...
FHWUP
FHWUP
FHWUP
...DELIVERED VIA PARACHUTE TO THEIR UNLUCKY RECIPIENTS.

BOOM
BOOM
BOOM

IT WAS A HALF-VICTORY, ANYWAY. RODAN ESCAPED. AGAIN.
AT LEAST WE'D IMMOBILIZED THE DINOSAUR—THE MONSTER TOYKO HAD HIRED US TO DEAL WITH.
COULDN'T WE HAVE AT LEAST TRIED THE ELEVATORS?
NO! NO ELEVATORS.
YOU ALL HEARD THAT EVERY TIME ONE OF THESE NEW MONSTERS POPS UP THERE'S A BIG DIE-OFF ELSEWHERE? HEARD IT WAS SQUIRRELS THIS TIME.
I'M WONDERING HOW MUCH LONGER WE CAN KEEP THIS UP.
YOU ALL SAW IT TODAY. THE BEAM DOESN'T WORK ON ALL OF THEM.
SQUIRRELS, MAN. I REALLY LIKED SQUIRRELS.
AND DOESN'T IT BOTHER YOU, BOXER, THAT WE NEVER HEARD ABOUT WHERE THE GOVERNMENTS PUT THESE THINGS?
I COULD GIVE A RAT'S ARSE. HAVE YOU FORGOTTEN THAT WE'RE, OH, I DON'T KNOW, SEVEN BILLION RICHER?
COME TO THINK OF IT, LET'S GO BUY A BAR SOMEWHERE AND GET STUPID DRUNK.

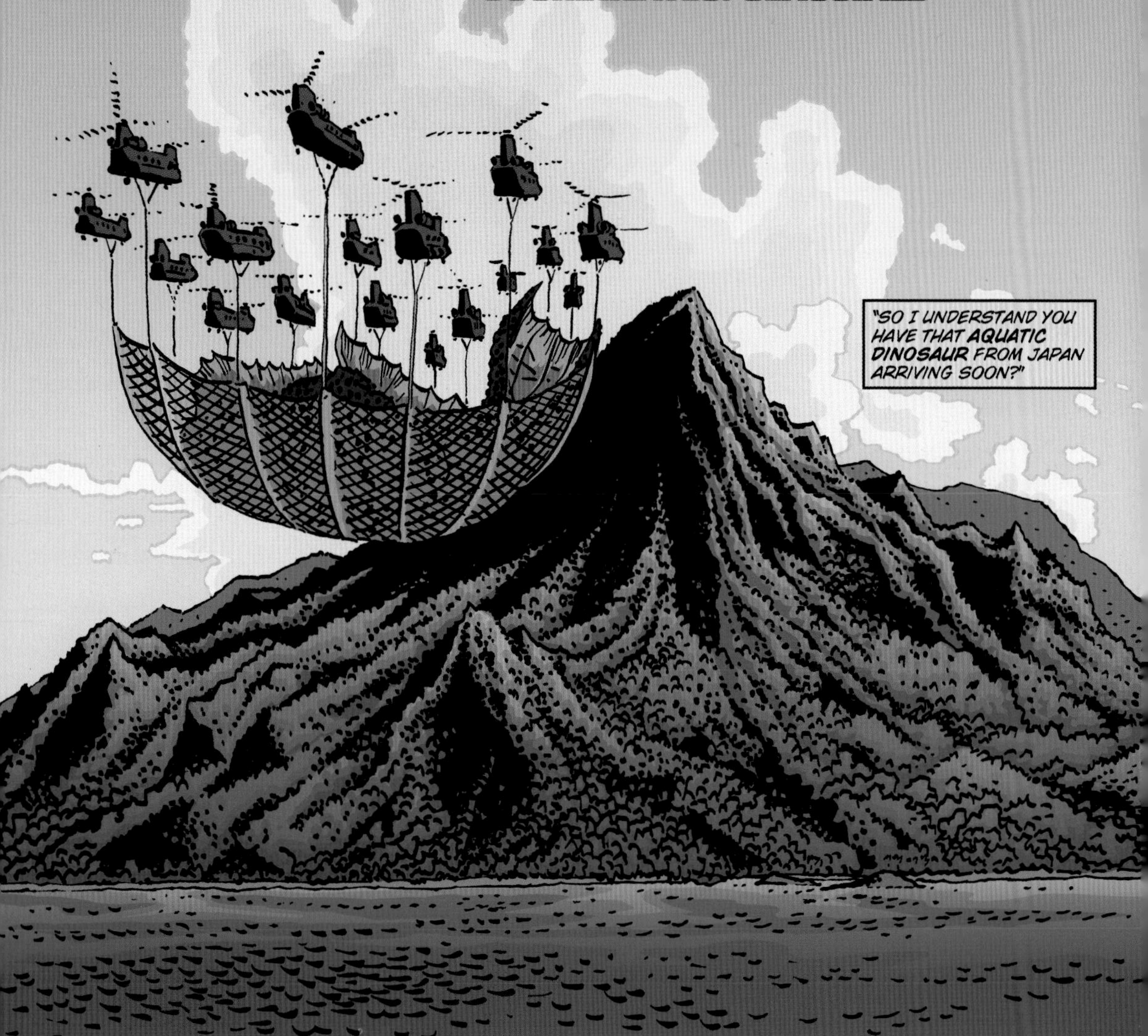
HUNT ATOLL, SOUTH PACIFIC OCEAN,
A.K.A. "MONSTER ISLAND."
COORDINATES: CLASSIFIED
"SO I UNDERSTAND YOU HAVE THAT AQUATIC DINOSAUR FROM JAPAN ARRIVING SOON?"

WE'RE CALLING IT TITANOSAURUS. IT'S IMPORTANT TO THINK OF THE BRANDING POTENTIAL.
HELL, THEY'RE ALL MONSTERS TO ME. ANYWAY, YOU WERE EXPLAINING HOW YOU KEEP THEM DOCILE.

WE APPROPRIATED, THEN MODIFIED, A DEVICE CALLED A HEADACHE BEAM.
I'M FAMILIAR WITH IT FROM THE CIA REPORT. YOU TELLING ME CLAIRE PLANGMAN JUST GAVE IT TO YOU?
NO. I SAID WE APPROPRIATED IT.
WELL, THAT'S ONE WAY TO SAVE A BUCK. WHICH IS GOOD, BECAUSE THE MEMBER NATIONS ARE GRUMBLING ABOUT HOW MUCH THIS BOXER FELLOW CHARGES.
THEY'RE HOPING FOR A SERIOUS RETURN ON THEIR SIZEABLE INVESTMENTS.
YOU CAN TELL THE MEMBER NATIONS THAT TAMED AND WEAPONIZED CREATURES OF THIS MAGNITUDE ARE PRICELESS.
ESPECIALLY WHEN WE CAPTURE HIM.

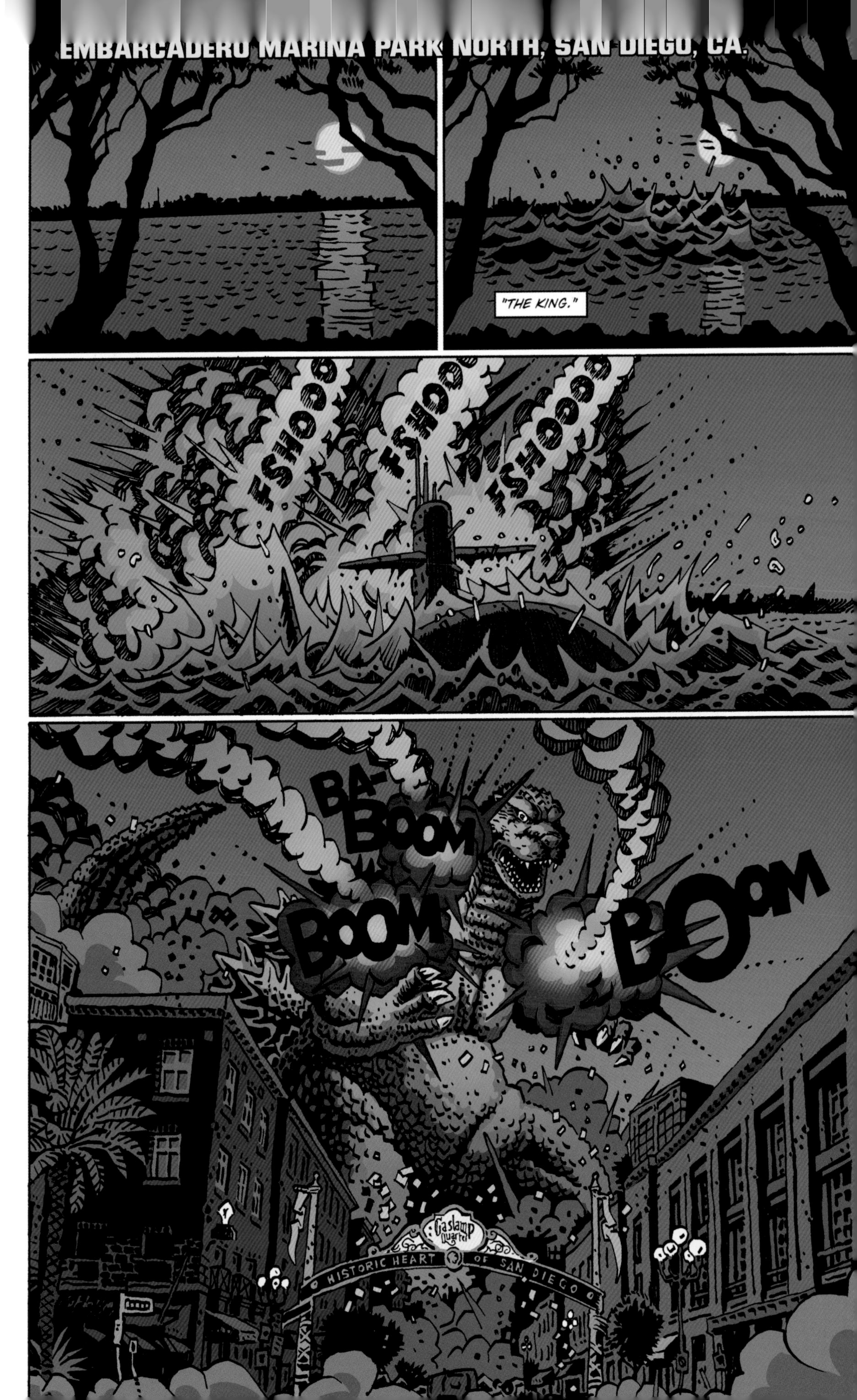
EMBARCADERO MARINA PARK NORTH, SAN DIEGO, CA.
"THE KING."
FSHOOO
FSHOOO
FSHOOO
BA-BOOM
BOOM
BOOOM
Gaslamp Quarter
HISTORIC HEART OF SAN DIEGO

FWOOOM

EXHIBIT HALL A

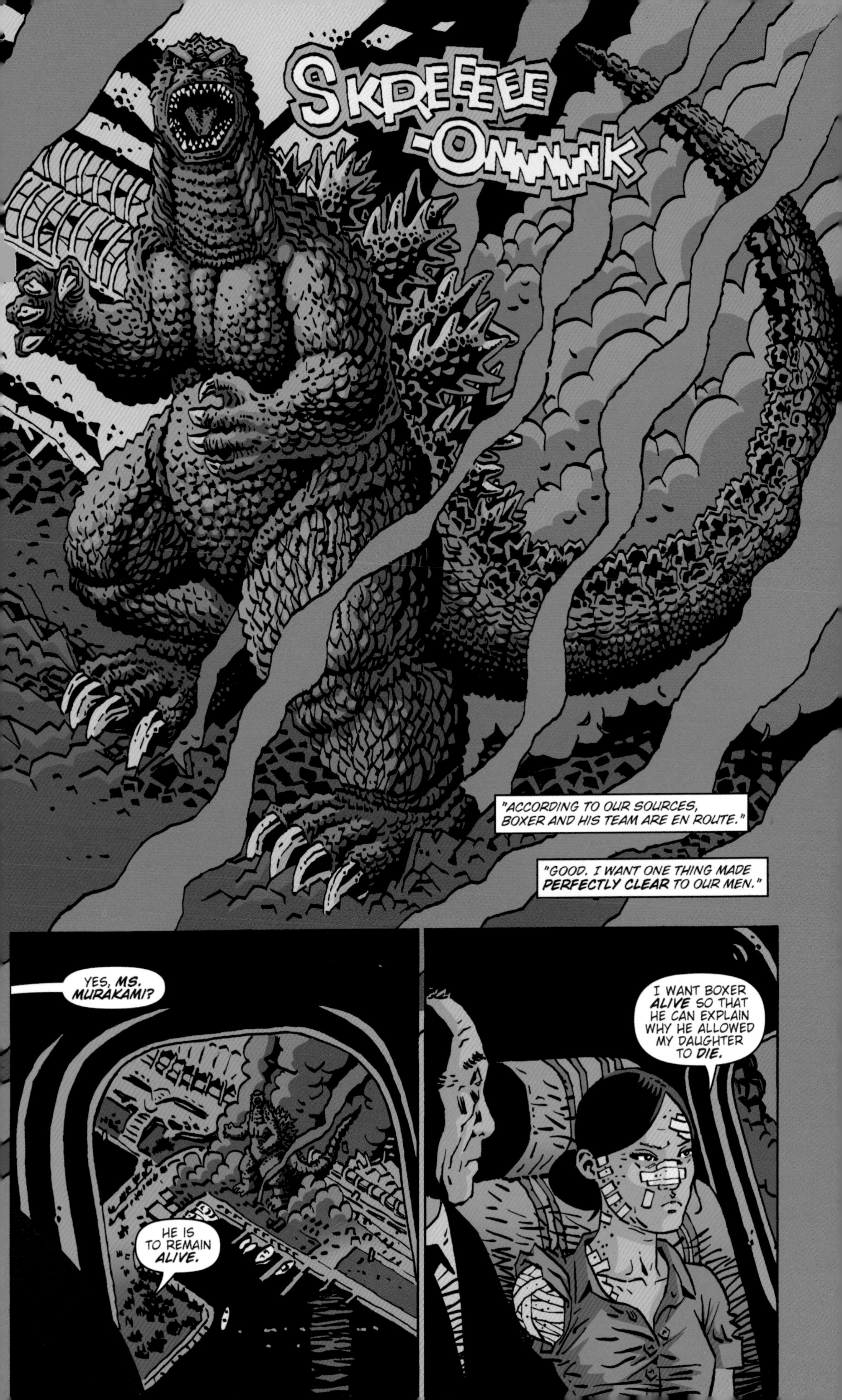
SKREEEEE -ONNNNNK
"ACCORDING TO OUR SOURCES, BOXER AND HIS TEAM ARE EN ROUTE."
"GOOD. I WANT ONE THING MADE PERFECTLY CLEAR TO OUR MEN."
YES, MS. MURAKAMI?
HE IS TO REMAIN ALIVE.
I WANT BOXER ALIVE SO THAT HE CAN EXPLAIN WHY HE ALLOWED MY DAUGHTER TO DIE.

I'M TELLING YOU, IF THE HEADACHE BEAM WAS USELESS AGAINST THAT DINOSAUR, THERE'S NO WAY IT'LL WORK ON GODZILLA. THE PHYSIOLOGY IS TOO—
—HEY, ARE YOU EVEN LISTENING TO ME?
CLAIRE, I WAS LYING EARLIER. IT'S NOT ABOUT THE MONEY. NEVER WAS.
THE MONEY'S ONLY GOOD FOR ONE THING, AND THAT'S BUYING ENOUGH BOMBS AND WEAPONS AND TECHNOLOGY AND POINTY STICKS AND WHATEVER THE HELL ELSE IT TAKES TO PUT THAT DAMNED THING DOWN FOR GOOD.
YOU ASKED BEFORE HOW MUCH LONGER WE CAN GO ON?
SKREEEEEE-
-ONNNNNK
"WE DON'T STOP UNTIL GODZILLA'S DEAD."
TO BE CONTINUED IN

ART GALLERY

ART BY MATT FRANK

ART BY TONY HARRIS

ART BY RYAN KELLY
COLORS BY RICO RENZY

ART BY JEFF ZORNOW

ART BY JEFF ZORNOW

ART BY JEFF ZORNOW